I0220848

HONING A
CHAMPION

*My Pandemic Journey From
White Belt To Achieving Black Belt*

HAON SEBASTIAN AUSTIN CAMPBELL

HONING A CHAMPION

My Pandemic Journey From
White Belt To Achieving Black Belt

HAON SEBASTIAN AUSTIN CAMPBELL

HONING A CHAMPION

My Pandemic Journey From White Belt To Achieving Black Belt

HAON'S
Little Flash

我
是
甘嵘

Haon Sebastian Austin Campbell

HCE Publishing

Haon Campbell Enterprise, LLC

Lean Mobile Apps, LLC

Las Vegas, U.S.A.

Second Edition 2020

WARNING: Martial arts practice is a rigorous and potentially savage struggle.

Training ventures should be done under the instruction of a proficient practitioner.

The material contained in this book is for research purposes only. The reader assume all risk of training and absolves the author and publisher of liability.

Cover Photo: A young Hoan Campbell training during his journey to black belt.

Editorial Assistance by Even Me, LLC

Edited by Malik Williams

ISBN: 987-1-953641-02-1

HOLD THE LINE

MORE MAXIMUM !

"

Rest in Peace Kwan Jang Nim Beaudoin

Tang Soo!

Thank You Kwan Jang Nim Wesley C. Jenkins Dan #18983

for your support and encouragement.

I hope to reflect your words "Continue to Grow so you can Glow."

In some small way, I hope to show in this book,

that I've got the glow as I continue to grow.

Tang Soo Sir!

I'm grateful to everyone that has helped me along the way.

Thank You to every Sa Bom Nim, Kyo Sa Nim, Sun Beh Nim

and Fu Beh Nim, gamsahabnida
감사합니다

Tang Soo!

Grateful to focus and learn !

Tang Soo Do

PENCRAFT AWARDS
WINNER
2020
LITERARY EXCELLENCE

Thank you to Mr. Malik Williams, Even Me LLC, HCE Publishing & the Lean Mobile Apps team, Alva, Joyce & Po for all your supportive advice, guidance and consistent wisdom.

I'm grateful to Hannah Jacobson for your most insightful, conveniently brilliant system.

Last but not least, I'm grateful to the Pencraft Awards selection committee for picking my book as an award winner for literary excellence.

I'm humbled by this award. The team work has inspired me.

I look forward to working with the team on my series of illustrated books to come.

Royal
Dragonfly
Book Award
SM
WINNER

As a 2020 Royal Dragonfly Book Award Winner, I am thankful for the time time effort and consideration of Story Monsters, LLC. I am well aware that this award tells readers and industry professionals that what I'm offering is a highly acclaimed work. This award in particular makes me think about my school.

I wrote this book during the 2020 Pandemic. I miss having fun with my friends and being in school so much. I'm amazed at the work educators have done during this pandemic. I'm also respectfully grateful for all the extra help my teachers have given me in particular. From recommendation letters to club leaders organizing, I take pride in knowing that I attend school filled with leaders. I take this time to acknowledge my teachers, and school staff whom also inspired me to learn.

My haiku at the beginning and end of the book are bookends to who I am. At the same time, without your guidance, I wouldn't know what a haiku is. I'm much obliged to the Royal Dragonfly Book Awards team for selecting my work. I'm modestly motivated to do more by the entire educational team at Dr. Samuel A. Mudd for working with me. Go Fierce Dragons!

TABLE OF CONTENTS

FOREWORD

●●●●●●

My journey into martial arts began over 20 years ago in 1998. I was an online marketing optimization manager for a publicly traded startup. It was a unicorn, meaning it was a company started in a garage that became worth a billion dollars.

At the time, we had many amenities and lots of playtime. We worked hard, and we played hard. Sixty hour work weeks were a regular occurrence. But within those sixty hours were many moments of creative time.

As part of that creative time, I started training in Wing Chun at the office. We practiced for an hour or two daily for roughly a year. I have dabbled in martial arts on and off for most of that time since 2000. I didn't have an appreciation for martial arts until watching Haon.

When I started to take martial arts seriously, my son took it more seriously. Many training sessions Hoan was used to help hone the craft of others. He was out in front of all of us to illustrate stances. He was utilized as an example to show others (black belts and gup members) how to have a spirit yell.

I remember his impressive first win. I vividly recall his first loss. After the loss, he walked away with nothing but hurt emotions and a trail of tears that a simple hug couldn't comfort. Thanks to all the tears streaming down his face, he realized he had to do better.

There was no pressure from me to ever compete again for any reason. He realized that he wouldn't place in an out-of-town tournament who didn't know who he was or his instructor. All he could do would be to demonstrate with discipline; what his instructors have taught him.

Over the years, there were a lot of costs in this process. We spent countless hours traveling. The flights, rental cars, hotel accommodations, food, and incidental expenses, not to mention all the years of dedicated practices; all totals into the tens of thousands. In some cases we spent significant money to walk away with absolutely nothing.

Haon was crushed by losses, especially when we didn't even get a "thank you" or "nice to see you" from the judges. That is pretty cold when it comes to kids under 10 years old. What it means is, humbly, you can't go in haphazard or without a plan. It would be best if you went in having practiced hard, trained well, and always kept your discipline.

At this moment, he is a nine-year-old black belt. What isn't understood is the patience learned, criticism received, and sacrifice made as a beginner. The frustration that happened regularly to learn the basics. I would be remiss if I didn't mention the will power to persevere through that frustration as he achieves his goals.

Fundamentally this martial art taught him to set and achieve goals. There is a virtue in learning to keep your discipline. When you don't lose control even when justified, you build character.

The book doesn't discuss the injuries from shin splints to losing a big full toenail during training. I would be negligent not to honor the personal training, outside training, doctor visits and rehab treatments; were all a part of the physical investment.

What you might get as a part of this book is an inkling of self-doubt. This book is here to show you the benefit of the persistence that it takes to pass that self-doubt en route to your reward. We are giving the iceberg tip about the hard work, dedication, and pain it took to achieve this goal.

As a parent, I couldn't, and I wouldn't buy a belt. I couldn't, and I wouldn't take a test for him. I couldn't and I wouldn't even ask an instructor when he would move to the next level. I work with him through his struggle. I did let him know his choices do determine his outcome. I also let him know right or wrong in his results; he is not alone. I cannot, and I would not influence the committee to make the test harder or softer.

Haon committed to setting and achieving goals. When he commits to a goal mentally, the goal isn't going away. He might not talk about it often, but it's a goal that he harbors deep within the recesses of his heart. He laborers to achieve that goal. Sacrifices for that goal. His self-defined goals are a part of his journey. The martial arts instructors have fostered the capacity to become an award-winning student, successful athlete, goal-driven child, and best-selling author.

I'm happy, proud, and humbled that he is my youngest son.

Monty Campbell,
Cho Dan
Tang Soo Do
1st Degree Black Belt

Martial Arts Is Life
Learning Breathing Centers Strength
Wisdon's Discipline

INTRODUCTION

● ● ● ● ● ● ● ●

This book shares some of my journey but not the entire story. I have dedicated this book to answer a few basic questions. Usually, my mom and dad get these questions. Sometimes I get a few too. We get questions such as:

● When did he start?

● How old is he?

● What did it take to get your black belt?

● Why did you choose Tang Soo Do?

● What is it like to be a black belt?

● Where have you competed?

● Do you go to tournaments?

● When did you start competing?

● How often do you train?

● How often do you practice?

● Is it vital to "x"?

"Who I am", is something I have to answer to every judge I've met. I have to introduce myself. Here is how my introduction goes in strong voice from my attention stance:

> *"Good evening, judges! My name is Haon Campbell! I study Tang Soo Do At (my school), under (my instructors)! With your permission, I would like to demonstrate to you (my form)! May I begin?"*

That is the brief introduction I give every time. It changes with some advanced forms because I must speak to the meaning of the hyung (form). In some cases, I provide more information about my instructors. It took awhile for me to get comfortable introducing myself. This introduction is how I'm introducing myself to you.

How long it took for me to get here, cannot be summed up in 5 years. For me, it was more than half my life. How many things have you done for more than half of your life? Although this is my story, this book is not about me. This book is really about sharing my family, friends, and the fun I had along the way.

Even in the middle of COVID-19, we were able to have fun while remaining safe and healthy. I was disappointed when we couldn't practice in the dojo because of the coronavirus. I've learned and grown since that time. I continued to practice and train while quarantined. When things opened back up, I practiced as we learned to do training with masks and social distancing.

This book is not just about earning a black belt at the start of the shutdown. It's partially about continuing to train at home despite the pandemic. More importantly, you should practice regardless of what is going on around you, just like a tournament's chaos. The focus is to demonstrate your discipline. My Kwan Jang Nim calls it "Tiger Discipline." One other phrase he speaks to is "Grow and Glow." As I grow, I strive to work in that "Glow." My family uses the theme "I Got The Glow" to refer to walking in that energy at that moment.

I am grateful to work and train as I go with the "Glow" to go where the path leads me. This book is also about just continuing the journey despite blood, sweat, and tears happening along the way. This book is my passion. I hope you enjoy reading it.

I look forward to connecting with you on your journey.

Tang Soo!

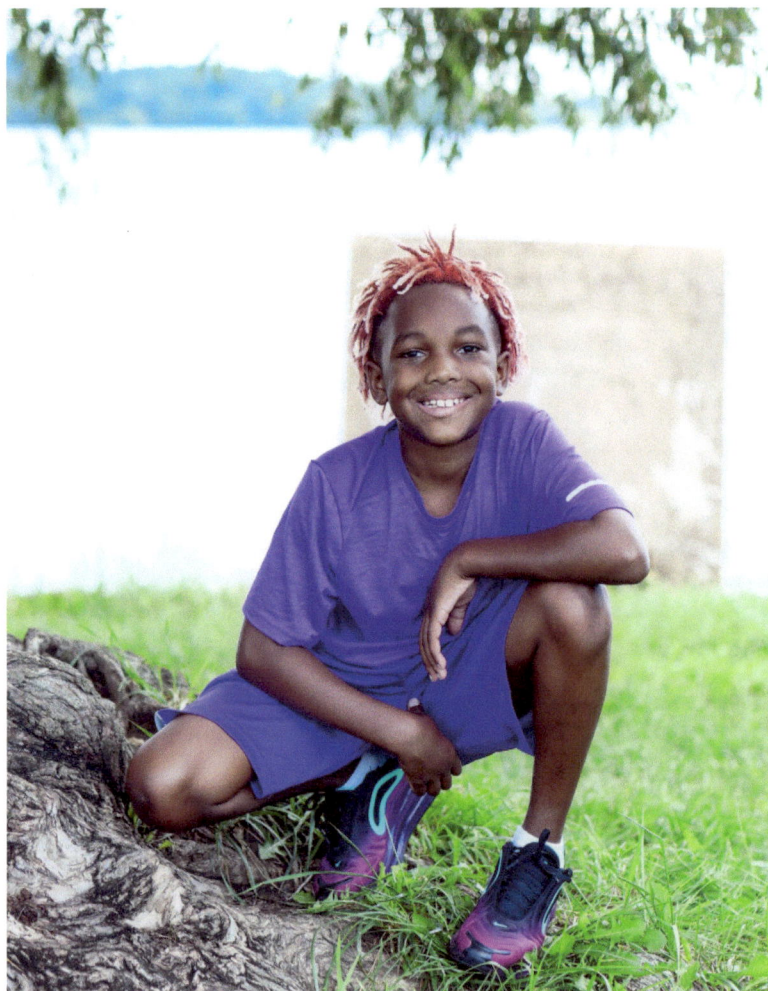

CHAPTER 1
FADE TO BLACK

"A journey of a thousand miles begins with a single step." - Lao Tzu

(Lao Tzu (AKA Laozi) is a central figure in Chinese culture who was an ancient Chinese philosopher. Laozi is commonly translated as "Old Master". the founder of philosophical Taoism. Laozi is claimed by both the emperors of the Tang dynasty, and modern people of the Li surname as a founder of their lineage.)

HAON'S JOURNEY BEGINS

On March 13th, 2020, my school closed. I didn't get a chance to compete in my MESA tournament. I had been practicing for months to compete with schools around the region in math, scientific studies, engineering, and artistic design. But my big question was about Karate.

"Greetings, my name is Haon. I practice Tang Soo Do at Tiger Do Jang under the chief instruction of Master Janice Scroggins with the guidance of Kwan Jang Nim Wesley C Jenkins, Dan Number 18983."

That phrase is in my head and heart because I've said it thousands of times in competition. It has been modified slightly by shifts here and there, but the content primarily stayed the same. As a whole, the change was for which form I planned to demonstrate.

I've performed hundreds of open hand forms and weapons forms in regional, national, World Dang Soo Do Unions, and open competition. I can hear it with each beat of my heart. As the time for playing ends, I stand in front of the judges, I take a deep breath, and the seriousness begins.

In the process of competing, I've learned many things about myself and my competition. Just like my name, many people don't know what Tang Soo Do is. In the movie "Karate Kid," Cobra Kai is the Tang Soo Do version of Karate. The source elements, and its chief film instructor's background are in the military art in Tang Soo Do.

At the core, I am here to share what it was like for me to go from watching Karate on TV to having the opportunity to be on stage in front of five-hundred people in the spotlight to do Karate. My journey began when I was four years old and had a Christmas break from day camp.

CHAPTER 2

BECOMING A MARTIAL ARTIST

"It does not matter how slowly you go as long as you do not stop." - Confucius

(He espoused the well-known principle "Do not do unto others what you do not want done to yourself", the Golden Rule. He is also a traditional deity in Daoism.)

RECEIVING THE WHITE BELT

At four, my mom and dad noticed that I liked the Power Rangers. Mom thought I might be interested in martial arts. She told me that she used to pick up my cousins from Tiger Do Jang aftercare.

My first practice was on a Saturday in January. I was scared to come out of the locker room. Cho Dan Bo Olivia showed me how to bow; then she took my hand and walked me onto the floor. She showed me basic kicks, and after a while, I wasn't scared anymore.

I HAD A LOT TO LEARN

I was a white belt for 12 months. For all those months, I learned:

- Form one,
- Stances,
- Kicking
- Punching.

Saturdays were my only practice day; then, I moved onto summer camp. In summer camp, we practiced Karate every single day. I learned form one.

I learned Saturday classes are the same as our weekday classes, just that it's on a different day. On Saturday, we participate in:

- Sparring,
- Kicking drills
- Exercises.

It depends on what the Grand Master wants us to work on that day.

MEANING OF KARATE AS A WHITE BELT

On Saturday in groups, we would demonstrate basic kicks, punches, and everything you need to know from white belt to Cho Dan Bo. I could see what I needed to learn by watching others.

We would Ahn Jo (sit down), and watch what each different rank practiced unders their Sun Beh Nim (senior member or senior student of the school).

We would all learn to start and finish class in korean by saying the following:

- Cha Ryut (Attention),
- Kuk Gi Bay Ray (Bow to the Flag),
- Ba Ro (Return),
- Muk Nyum (Meditation),
- Ba Ro (Return),

- Cha Ryut (Attention),
- Kwan Jang Nim Kay Kyung Yet (Bow to the Founder of the school),
- Cha Ryut (Attention),
- Sa Bom Nim Kay Kyung Yet (Bow to Master Instructor).

The process continued until you reached Cho Dan Bo (black belt candidate).

My dad and I walked to class one Saturday; but, the doors were locked. Another parent came and told us that there was a tournament.

Then my dad asked, "Do you want to go to the tournament"?

I said, "Yes."

I really didn't know what I said yes to do. I had no clue what a tournament was at all. I just knew the people I knew were there and I wanted to be there too. For me, it wasn't about competition or medals and trophies. It was about having fun.

Several months later, I competed in my first tournament. It was "Kim's Karate Tournament" in York, PA. We went, and I saw all of my friends.

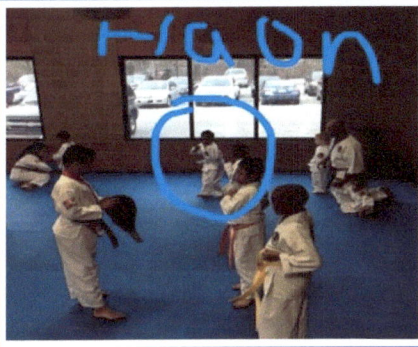

I did my best. I didn't win. Grand Master Jenkin's gave me a t-shirt that was signed. I received a participation medal. That t-shirt and medal was the first thing I hung in my trophy room.

WHAT I TOOK AWAY FROM MY 1ST TOURNAMENT

The shirt was too big for me to wear. I didn't know what to do with it. Then my parents installed a trophy room before I had any trophies. My parents put the t-shirt and medal in a shadow box. It was big and we didn't know where to put the shadow box cases. We decided to put it on the side of the wall.

My plan now was to start going to more tournaments. I didn't know what competitions were about, but I liked going. I thought each was just a one-time tournament and then no more tournaments.

When I started to go more often, I got to know the meaning of each competition. I learned who was having the contests and what time they began; most were 9 am. I started to read the times and dates. The black belts dressed up for tournaments; so, I did too.

Tournaments were happening on Saturdays. They were like Saturday practice at Tiger. We demonstrated what we knew. We showed what we learned to the judges.

It meant kicking, punching, and blocking as I learned to protect myself from anything around me. Some parts of the world are dangerous, and I needed to learn to defend myself. I needed to know how to protect myself, which is why I practice Karate.

CHAPTER 3

COMPETING IN MARTIAL ARTS / GETTING EXPERIENCE

"People were asking me [before a fight], 'What's going to happen?,' " Tyson said. "They were talking about his style. 'He's going to give you a lot of lateral movement. He's going to move, he's going to dance. He's going to do this, do that.' I said, "Everybody has a plan until they get hit. Then, like a rat, they stop in fear and freeze.' " --Mike Tyson

(Former Undisputed World Heavyweight Boxing Champion and Creator of the stage play "Undisputed Truth.")

GETTING A PLAN FOR COMPETITION

T he Dennis Brown tournament was a little more challenging than the other matches because sometimes things aren't always fair; I had to keep kicking my opponent even after I had an exact point. Even though the rule said no contact, sometimes the ring judges change the rules. My Grand Master said best "You need to get comfortable being uncomfortable."

I practice continuous sparring where we don't just seek to score a quick point. I remember practicing with my Sa Bom Nim to get ready for tougher opponents. This practice paid off when it came to this tournament. The judges wanted to see clear contact, so they could see what I was doing and count the points.

I placed second in forms. I needed it to improve my forms and stances. In the "iron person" event, we did everything from kicks to punches and situps for two minutes.

I was a white belt with a yellow stripe when I participated in the "Iron Person" challenge. We had to do push-ups, situps, crunches, and three types of kicks.

Next up was forms and sparring, and although I was interested, we hadn't started my training in weapons yet, so I couldn't compete in the weapons category.

I didn't know what to expect from sparring. This was my first time

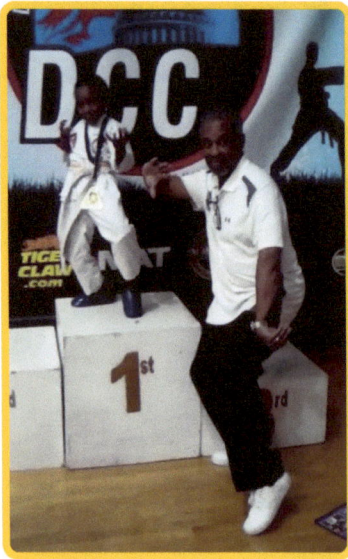

sparring with someone who had a completely different style. Their belt was silk. The uniform was black. They had a completely different bow. Everything was new to me.

At the end of the tournament, I won 1st place twice and second place once. I got punched in the mouth and my plan worked. We took pictures, and I got to meet GrandMaster Brown. He was friendly, and when he saw my tiger claw pose, he said: "Wait a minute, let me get my stance," and this was the result.

HOW DID IT FEEL TO WIN

How it felt to win was great. It felt like it was a one time experience. The trophy looked terrific, and it was metal, so I liked it when I earned it. I was planning on going onto more tournaments to see if I could achieve even more trophies.

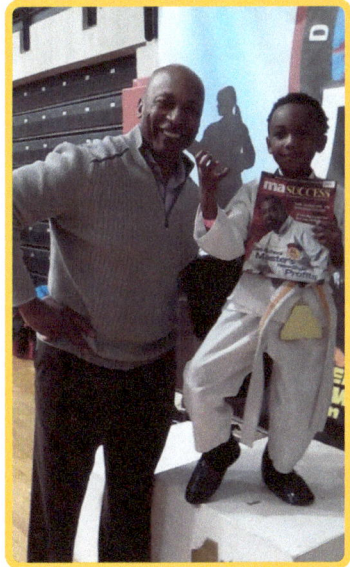

I relived every moment over and over again watching the video my parents took. It was cool to see the kicks and punches. This was also the beginning of the youtube channel my family eventually set up for my journey.

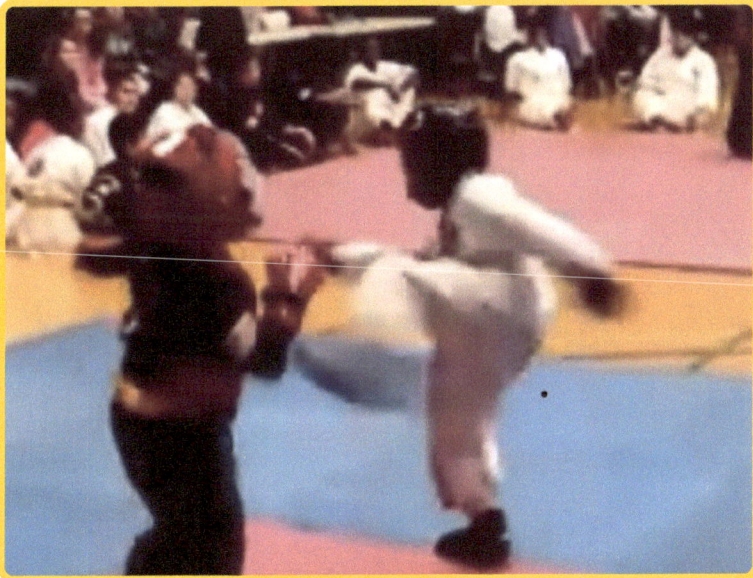

CHAPTER 4

WINNING MY FIRST NATIONAL CHAMPIONSHIP

In 1968, I fought and won the world middleweight karate championship by defeating the world's top fighters. I then held that title until 1974, when I retired undefeated.-- Chuck Norris

(Actor Tang Soo Do Grand Master & Practitioner)

我

I GOT THE GLOW

甘榮

GOING FOR A
NATIONAL CHAMPIONSHIP

Tiger Do Jang shuts down when we have the National Tournament. The school doesn't shut down any other time.

FINDING OUT ABOUT USGTA

I learned that Tiger Dojang is a part of the United States Goodwill Tang Soo Do Association (USGTA). Though I felt ready, I knew I needed to practice more on my stances and kicks. I've always watched the black belts and knew I needed to improve everything to not get cheated. I wanted to do my best.

HAON'S LITTLE FLASH

Ki hap(spirit yell) as loud as possible. I had to practice and learn my forms so that I knew them with my eyes closed. I had to lift my knee when I kicked. My pace was too fast, so I had to slow down and add more power.

NATIONALS

I found out what a National Champion is, and I was ready. I didn't know what to expect, but I just kept thinking it couldn't be more challenging than Dennis Brown. I knew it would be fun.

我是甘嵘 HAON'S *Little Flash*.

So I trained, practiced hard, and set a goal to go. I asked my mom and dad. This tournament was why the school was closed when we walked to the dojo on that Saturday over a year ago.

I ended up winning the championship in front of a wall of my black belt instructors. That kick captured during that tournament became my logo.

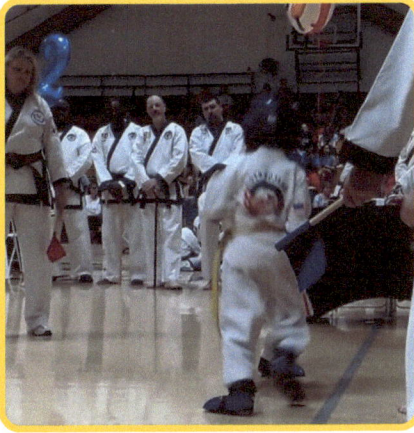

REGIONAL CHAMPIONSHIP

I learned the Regional Championship was in Connecticut, just like Nationals. I got to meet my Grand Master's Grand Master. Before I met him, I was clueless about him.

COMPETING FOR MY GRAND MASTER'S GRAND MASTER

I did the breaking, forms, and sparring. I earned second place in hyung (forms), received first place in breaking and sparring. After the tournament was over, my Grand Master told me to step aside. He instructed me to meet somebody, so I did. I didn't know who it was, but then my Grand Master said

to me that it was his Grand Master. I didn't know what to say, I met him in shock. After the tournament, my Kwan Jang Nim described Kwan Jang Nim Beaudoin and told me more about him.

MY GRAND MASTER'S GRAND MASTER

On May 12th in 1963, Grand Master Beaudoin tested and earned his first-degree black belt at Incheon, Korea, while serving in the military. Dr. Beaudoin founded the school my school's Grand Master attended when he was twelve. Here is where he first learned the martial art I came to love.

When I met Kwan Jang Nim Beaudoin, he was an 8th Degree black belt. Grandmaster Robert E. Beaudoin achieved his promotion to 8th Dan's rank at the 2010 World Championship in Greensboro, North Carolina. This monumental event marks the first time that Grand Master Jae C. Shin promoted one of his students to the title of Kwan Chang Nim.

CHAPTER 5

BECOMING A GRAND CHAMPION

"In the old days we trained Karate as a martial art, but now they train Karate as a gymnastic sport. I think we must avoid treating Karate as a sport - it must be a martial art at all times! Your fingers and the tips of your toes must be like arrows, your arms must be like iron. You have to think that if you kick, you try to kick the enemy dead. If you punch, you must thrust to kill. If you strike, then you strike to kill the enemy. This is the spirit you need in order to progress in your training." - Choshin Chibana

(founder of Kobayashi Shorin-ryu Karate)

GETTING TO COMPETE WITH CHAMPIONS

After Regionals' I learned to be loud with my ki hap. It was one main improvement I made for the Capital Classic's Tournament.

At this one tournament in Greenbelt, Maryland my Teacher Mr. Mackell attended. I was surprised and happy. My nerves were extra high this time.

MY FAVORITE TEACHER WATCHING ME COMPETE

Where some art forms add:

- Flips
- Slow movements
- Music
- Nunchucks or
- Throwing bo staff in the air

I had to compete hard because they were doing crazy stuff like spinning, catching, and flipping bongs.

I learned to be creative. I practice punching moving targets on my own in my training room.

Nothing was ever guaranteed. I just had to do my best. I worked hard and showed up. I practiced outside of the training. I trained six days a week. Most of those days I trained twice-a-day.

I practiced through rain sleet and snow. It didn't matter what the weather or situation was, I was there. The only thing that changed things was the 2020 Pandemic, and even then I practiced via Zoom.

When it came to getting ready for a tournament, I never had to get ready, I was training like I was ready. Every practice was a competition to me. I wanted to win at practice. I wanted to be better than myself. I wanted to be a Grand Champion.

I competed against all that and won. When I found out what a Grand Champion was, I set it as a goal. I wanted to be the best of the best.

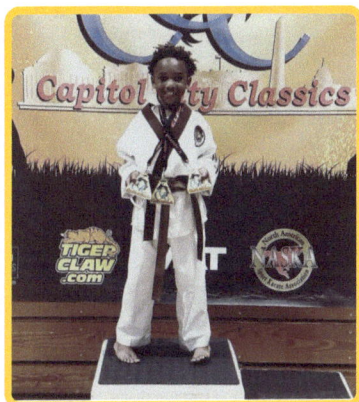

I trained even harder. I learned all the things judges looked for even before you demonstrate a form. I started to get even more focused after that first place.

I knew the judges watch you before you start your hyung and after you finish it. I began to try and put my style into the form so I can win the Grand Championship.

COMPETING FOR GRAND CHAMPION WITH BLINDFOLD

To my astonishment, it worked. When I was a brown belt, I was shocked by this victory. I didn't know what to say or do. I did my best, and it worked out. I was humbly grateful to my instructors and Sensei Dennis Brown for his tournament. To beat all the champions from a white belt up to a black belt candidate was a blessing.

CHAPTER 6

TRAVELING FROM COAST TO COAST WITH FAMILY FOR FUN

"However beautiful the strategy,
you should occasionally look at the results"
-Sir Winston Churchill

In California, the rules were a surprise because they told us we couldn't kick to the head. I adapted, and after doing it once. They gave me a warning. Then, I won in sparring.

When you travel and compete in tournaments, you learn more about the community where you go. In competing outside of your comfort zone, you learn to get comfortable being uncomfortable.

"Get comfortable being uncomfortable" Grand Master Jenkins says all the time. I've learned to say it whenever I'm nervous.

COMPETING WITH SENIOR BELTS TWICE MY AGE

In kata (Japanese for hyung) and weapons, I competed with thirteen-year-old advanced students. I was six at the time. I thought they were all going to kill me. I won first place in weapons but second place in forms.

LEARNING IN TOURNAMENTS WITH FRIENDS AND FAMILY

We picked him up from his house and then were on the plane. We landed and went to the Enterprise to rent this big truck. That night, we met up with our friends and instructors at a lobby in the hotel.

Then that night we had a big party in our suite with all kinds of snacks. We stayed up as long as we could, I passed out.

When we awoke, we were in a much cleaner room. My parents came in to clean much of the mess we had made. We then had to get ready for the day. I planned on doing my cane form at the national competition level. It's a black belt form that I've never seen an underbelt do.

WE PRACTICED A BIT BEFORE THE TOURNAMENT

As we got dressed in our uniforms, we did a little bit of practice. We make every effort not to change our routine entirely, just because we are away from the dojo. We have rituals, the training practice we have gotten down to a science. Each step before a tournament is to get in the right headspace to demonstrate skill.

USGTA NATIONAL TOURNAMENT

We arrived to the lobby and my cousin Caleb was in our hotel. We went to the tournament, which was probably like ten minutes away. In open hand hyung competition, we went up against somebody from another school; I don't know what to say; I didn't win. Then we did weapons; I didn't win there either.

So finally, we got to sparring. I earned the second-place medal. I watched Noah after my match. He had many sparring matches, and his opponents were huge. Somebody was trying to kick him out of the ring.

He fell, but then he jumped back up, and then Superman punched the guy to the ground. Even the judge said it was cool. We had a great time doing our best.

Nationals was a tough competition. It was one where the competitors all have trained just as hard as we have. We learned it isn't so easy to win. When your division has 15 competitors you learn to find a way to stand out.

I've learned from others what it was like to be a champion. I've been blessed to succeed in reaching my goals. In cases where I didn't, I learned too.

I learned to lose with dignity. I didn't throw down my helmet. I didn't swear at the judges even when I knew they were wrong. I didn't leave the floor before the winner was announced because I knew it wasn't me. I learned to honor the champion and then go have fun. Later I went to Atlantic City with Caleb; and, I won all the first places. This tournament was one where they made us remove our sparring gloves, and footgear was an option.

COMPETING IN ATLANTIC CITY, NEW JERSEY

So it was bare-knuckle boxing and kicking. One person accidentally kicked me in my lip, and I was bleeding, but I was okay. Fighting with no sparring gear is different. I learned from my Grand Master to "get comfortable being uncomfortable."

CHAPTER 7

WHAT HAS TANG SOO DO TAUGHT ME?

"Karate has no philosophy. Some people think that the tradition of Karate came from Buddhism and Karate has a connection with the absolute, space and universe, but I don't believe in that. My philosophy is to knock my opponent out, due to the use of only one technique. One finishing blow!" - Mikio Yahara

(former Japanese World Cup Champion, known for single-handedly defeating 34 local gangsters (yakuza), knocking out a mobster with a gun, and turning up for a competition with a knife wound.)

Tang Soo Do has been my passion for five years, and I have enjoyed each class. I have learned many things during my Tang Soo Do journey. Self-discipline, self-defense, and self-control each are traits Tang Soo Do has helped me continue to improve.

I've learned to connect my mind, body, and spirit making me stronger as I ki hap. I discover how to be more confident and work to get better at anything, especially when I think something is hard.

I've learned Tiger Dojang is a part of the United States Goodwill Tang Soo Do Association (USGTA). Though I felt ready, I knew I needed to practice more on my stances and kicks. I've always watched the black belts and knew I needed to improve everything so I would be at my absolute best. I always strive to do my very best.

I've learned that "Muk Nyum" is to meditate, and meditation helps center my focus. I've learned deep breathing is "Shum Shi Gi" and the reason that we do deep breathing because we do a lot of shallow breathing during practice. I've learned that the flag is "Kuk ki" and refers to both the Korean and American flags. I knew saying "Thank you" in Korean "Kam Sa Hap Ni Da", and saying "You're welcome" is "Chon ma ne yo."

I've learned all that Korean as I've had to open and close the class. It is a lot of pressure to organize the opening and closing of martial arts practice. I've learned how to do it thanks to Grand Master Sa Boh Nims, and the Black Belts.

I have been given more responsibility in the dojo as I teach others how to do forms. It is easy to be patient with them because others have been patient with me. I use my work ethic from practice as I do my school work, making me more focused and determined.

When I first started Tang Soo Do, I thought it was going to be just scary. I didn't want to come to the floor. I then learned it is a fun thing to do, but it became more demanding and profound as you reach higher belt ranks. I never expected the journey to a black belt would be comfortable. I have never worked so hard to achieve something before that I also know my family has done. Tang Soo Do has had a significant impact on my life, helping me be better at everything I attempt to do.

Before I started Tang Soo Do, I always watched power rangers and did kicks and punches for fun. Martial arts has taught me kicking with purpose and a clear direction. I've learned following rules is critical. It is not just the key to kicking and punching but following directions in life. Sometimes we are given instructions in class, and you must listen. Sometimes others are not listening. If you heard some teaching command, you should do what the class leader tells you.

Tiger Do Jang taught me the traits of honor, courage, strength, and patience. It is an honor to train with champions like Grand Master Jenkins and Sa Ban Nim Scroggins. I don't take lightly what senior instructors have achieved, and I know it was hard to achieve their

results. I know it takes courage to stand up and report. A performer can be in front of one person or five hundred; you still must be confident and as loud as you speak, and look the judges in the eye.

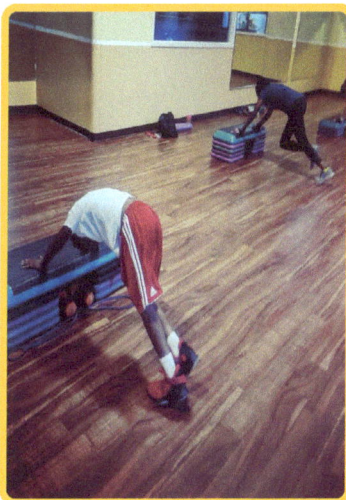

I've learned that it takes strength to do everything from push-ups to tiger crawls. After some practice, parts of my body hurt that I didn't know I had.

I've learned to be patient with myself when I don't know something instead of wanting to rush through it. I've learned and am still learning to breathe and take my time; it is not a race.

I've learned having the proper position of my footing allows me to have better control of my kick. Whether I am competing in a tournament or practicing at home, I've learned to do my best.

I'm also learning to be a good example for others. I'm not just doing this to get my own win, I want to help others reach their goals too. I want to help others the way the young leaders helped and inspired me.

I know that the process of training doesn't get easier over time. We just get more conditioned to the procedure. The procedure we do builds our character. Over time, I know as I follow the procedures laid out by Grand Master Jenkins and my instructors, I'll be fine.

Tiger Do Jang taught me perseverance and integrity. Tang Soo Do taught me that I had to persevere because if I quit, I would never reach the rank of black belt. Tang Soo Do also taught me how to respect others and be respectful around them, no matter the situation.

Tang Soo Do helped me compete in a Triathlon. I learned to ride my bike three days before the event. When I competed in the triathlon I got hurt. I was bloody but I didn't stop. Some Navy service members put a quick soft tourniquet on my leg and I got back on my bike. With blood dripping down my leg I let my parents know "I'm ok", as I dropped the bike and ran to finish the race.

Martial Arts taught me to never quit. The situation doesn't matter, what matters is how I respond.

I never wanted to quit, but sometimes I did feel like giving up for a moment. Tang Soo Do taught me everyone

has those moments and those moments pass. When you have a goal, you focus on that goal and not the moment.

I was blessed twice to compete in front of my Grandma. I won both times.

I've learned about competing. I knew just because you show up doesn't mean you will win. I've learned about different levels of championships. At the Regional Championship in Connecticut, I got to meet my Grand Master's Grand Master. Before I met him, I was clueless about him.

Competing in Front of My Grand Master's Grand Master wasn't hard. He made everyone feel

comfortable. He came and spoke to us and warmed us up before the competition. I competed in:

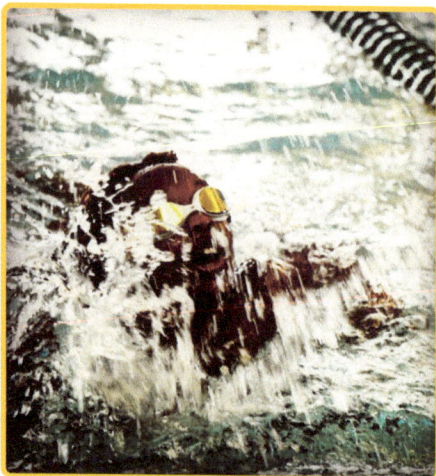

- Breaking (Gyeog pa),
- Forms (Hyung),
- and Sparring (Daelyeon).

I earned second place in forms. I got first place in breaking and sparring. After the tournament was over, my Grand Master Jenkins told me to step aside. He told me that I was going to meet somebody special, so I did. I didn't know who it was, but then my Grand Master said to me that it was his Grand Master. I didn't know what to say. I met him in shock. After the tournament, Kwan Jang Nim told me more about himself over the years.

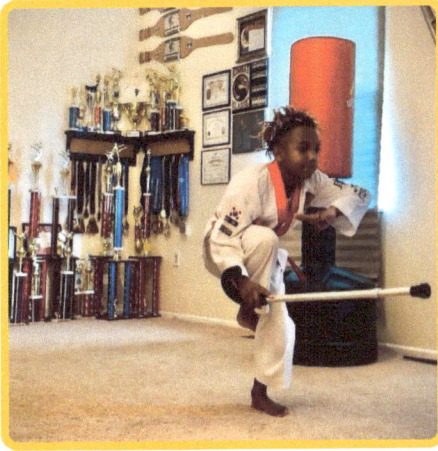

I've learned from meeting Grand Master Robert E. Beaudoin that he was a Ph.D, who focused on leadership. Grand Master Beaudoin also had a focus on stretching. I got a chance to stretch with him when I attended his tournament.

I was blessed to meet my Kwan Jang Nim's Kwan Jang Nim. I'm grateful for that opportunity. I have that picture with him of that meeting on my wall. I look at it whenever I practice in my training room. I also look at the shadow box of the medals from his tournament and the wood he signed for me.

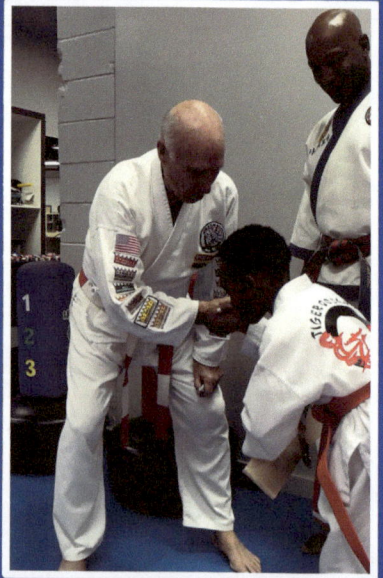

CHAPTER 8

WHAT DOES TANG SOO DO MEAN TO ME?

"Where there is preparation there is no fear"
-- Hwang Kee Founder of Soo Bak Do And Tang Soo
Do Mu Duk Kwan

The definition of Tang Soo Do means "the way of the open hand." This question is what I focused on in my black belt essay. I learned from Grand Master that Tang Soo Do means "The Way of the 'Tang' Hand" and "The Way of the 'China' Hand." I've also learned that our Tang Soo Do is traditional Moo Duk Kwan.

Moo Duk Kwaw means "School of Martial Virtue." I've learned that Moo Duk Kwan became Soo Bahk Do. From what I've learned, Soo Bahk Do, translated, means "Hand Striking Way." Soo Bahk Do in the martial arts sense means to forge a body towards gaining ultimate use of its faculties through intensive physical and mental training.

With all these different meanings, it can all get so confusing. I learned a lot meeting Grandmaster Hwang, 9th Dan, the current President of the U.S. Soo Bahk Do Moo Duk Kwan Federation. Grand Master Hwang is Grandmaster Kee Hwang's son. After Moo Duk Kwan and Tank Soo Do Founder Hwang Kee died on July 14th, 2002, his son Hwang Hyun-Chul (Jin Mun) was named his successor. His appointment was approved unanimously by the Board of Directors of the United States Soo Bahk Do Moo Duk Kwan Federation, Inc. as well as other chapters throughout the world.

What Tang Soo Do means to me is to keep learning. Even when I think I know something, I know there is more to learn about it. I didn't understand effective breathing until it was pointed out to me this year. I'm still working on proper breathing, which gives you more energy. I'm learning the sword form and many other elements of other open hand hyung.

My journey to learn just to grasp this martial art we call Tang Soo Do has increased the pace. I've learned the rich history of Tang Soo Do and know what I know is barely just the beginning.

Tang Soo Do is home for me. I'm more comfortable in a uniform than I am out of it. When I started, I didn't know how to write. Now I have written over five thousand words sharing my story.

In 2020, I wrote a 2,000 word essay to share what this black belt journey has been for me. I had to change the essay many times. I was nervous. My parents helped me print it off and edited it.

I've had to read that two thousand word essay aloud in front of my parents, grandparents, cousins, friends, and family, the black belts, the Sa Boh Nims, and my Grand Master. It was a lot of pressure and I choked up during the moment.

I will never have a fear of reading a book report in class with or without COVID-19. That 5,000 words original essay became this book.

Training at home during the pandemic was exciting. I got to be on Zoom calls with my friends and instructors. When we were able to connect outside the pandemic we had a great time (in spite of my facial expression).

We learned how to exercise and be safe with these masks. I even made some custom masks to go with my book.

For me, the journey wasn't ever about getting the black belt. The journey has always been about achieving my next goal. This most recent goal happens to be black, though. I didn't think I could write two thousand words. Now I don't think I will stop.

What Tang Soo Do means for me is learning how to do goal setting. So far, I've been pretty good at setting and achieving my goals. I've learned to manage my time. I've learned showing up on time is late.

I've learned on a basic level Tang Soo Do means "offensive-defensive strike." I've learned when we block, we block with purpose just as much as we would if we were punching. I've learned a soft block doesn't block anything. I've learned to bend my knee in my front stance because it was my knee's proper position when a hyung's demonstrated correctly.

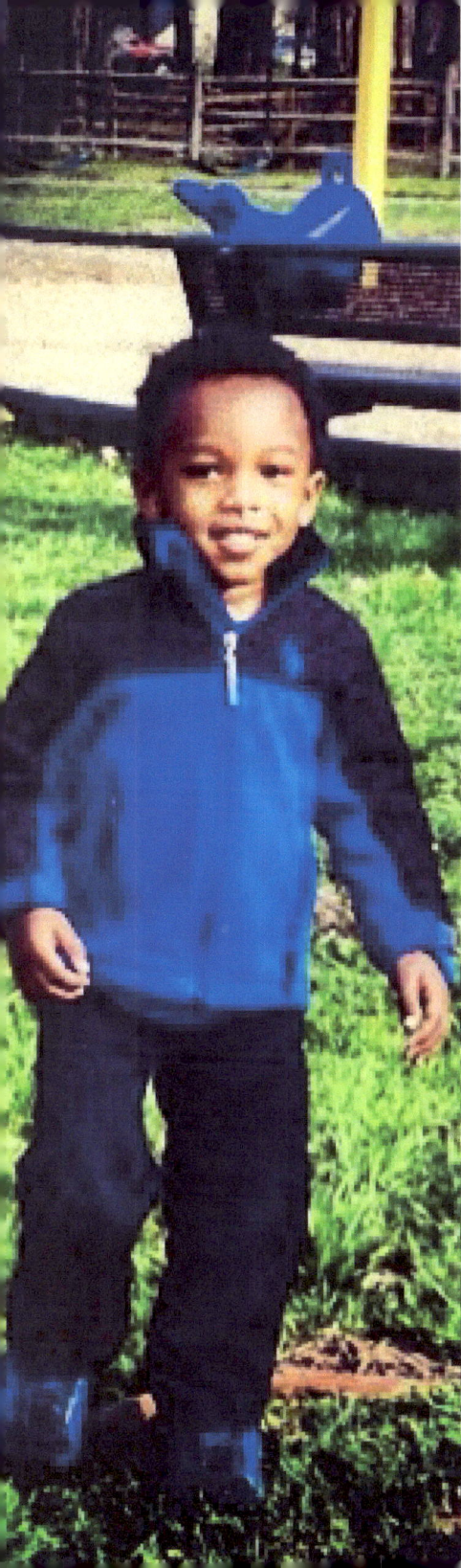

What Tang Soo Do means to me is having a neat, clean uniform at all times when practicing. I'll make sure my uniform is tight. I'm certain to keep my belt tied at all times. I've seen uniforms at other schools and during tournaments where people's clothing were a mess. When I started seeing their weak stances and messy clothing, I knew which arts, in particular, were not for me.

Tang Soo Do means showing others what I know and helping them to achieve their goals too. I can help people learn to tie belts or learn a form. I can help people learn how to present themselves at a tournament. I love to help teach and train new students as we learn to know what we know by teaching others. Sometimes I forget what I know and have to think about it, but I love what

I've learned, and I love being

able to share with other people. I'm thankful to my parents for this opportunity.

I keep an open mind and am willing to learn, and therefore I receive what is being shared in class and through life experiences. Tang Soo Do means "to protect myself at all times," whether armed or unarmed, because some people in this world might not know you and want to harm you. When I go swimming, I do my forms underwater, and I use the water's resistance against my body. Tang Soo Do has become a way of life for me, and I will never stop.

I have learned many things through Tang Soo Do. I now know hard work and perseverance aid us in accomplishing our goals. I learned discipline builds character. Sometimes people may doubt you, but you have to prove them wrong.

Tang Soo Do has helped me become strong not just in body but also

in my mind; it made me stronger, more confident, and a leader, so I work so hard in school.

When I started I remember how Cho Dan Bo Olivia and Major inspired me. They were helping me to become confident in the basics. I remember the day when they came back on a Saturday in April and they were Cho Dans (Black Belts). They were not Jr. Black Belts, they were black belts. They had their black belt uniform and were dressed just like all the other black belts.

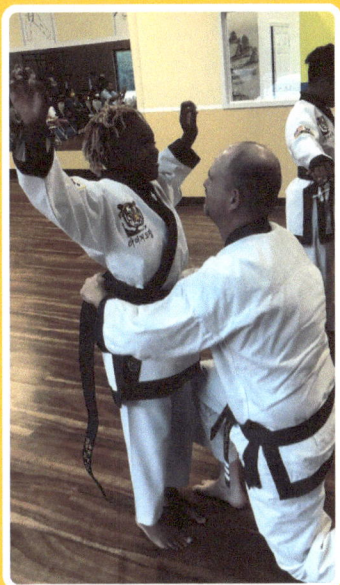

Fast forward, I now know what it's like to have a uniform that doesn't quite fit and feels heavy. Heavy not because of the weight, but because of greats that came before me like Cho Dan Olivia, Major, Sa Bum Nim Marcus, and Nur. They set the standard at a high level. Earning a black belt doesn't stop my journey to learn. I wanted to learn more.

I traveled from coast to coast to learn. I was blessed to meet some amazing people in my journey. I've been able to travel as far as Las Vegas to practice and train.

I wanted to know more about martial arts, so I asked my dad. I wanted to attend workshops to learn. Competing in open tournaments taught me not only the customs and courtesies of the Tang Soo Do way; but those of other styles as well, which is essential. For instance, the tradition of not turning your back to a Japanese style judge as it is a sign of disrespect.

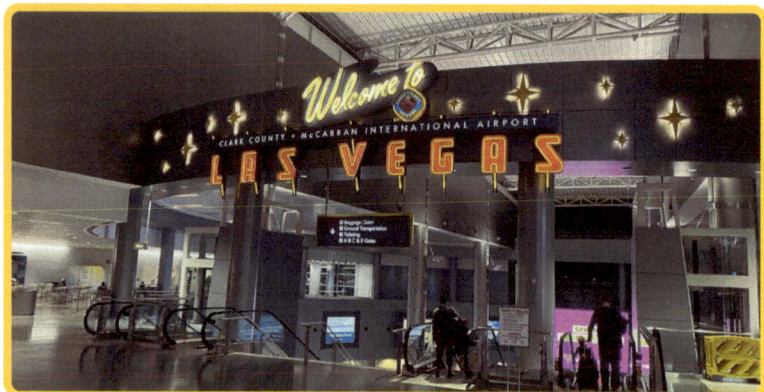

I learned a lot about "respect" in Tang Soo Do. Kwan Jang Nim Jenkin's say "Quality goes in before the belt goes on."

A black belt means continuously improving and becoming one with the forms. I will be able to teach sometimes as I've done before, so it just means to me that you are not quitting, doing your best at

all times. A blackbelt to me means to keep going when things are hard, because of times like South Carolina, where Hanshi Larry Isaac & the Dragon Society honored me as a champion's champion of the year. Hanshi Larry Isaac is a 10th-degree black belt and retired Recon Marine who teaches Okinawa Kenpo Karate and Kobudo. I'm blessed to be presented the trophy by Mr. Larry Isaac, who currently holds the following ranks:

- 10th Dan - Okinawa Kenpo-Kobudo Karate;

- 7th Dan - Okinawa-te;

- 5th Dan - Shorin-ryu Karate-Do;

- and 2nd Dan - Goshindo Karate-Do.

What becoming a blackbelt means to me? It means learning from great masters like Hanashi Isaac, who give back to their community with the dragon society.

Becoming a black belt to me means I am beginning my Master's journey. Earning my blackbelt after five years means I've completed my black belt journey. My thought is, as Grand Master says, "A black belt is just a white belt that never quit."

TIGERS EAT RED MEAT
TIGERS ROAR VERY LOUDLY
I AM A TIGER

www.ingramcontent.com/pod-product-compliance
Lightning Source LLC
Chambersburg PA
CBHW042128080426
42735CB00001B/3